I HEAR
THE TREES

UNTAMED POEMS
FROM MOTHER EARTH

FOR JOSEPH, FIONA AND ARLO

WELBECK

First published in Great Britain in 2025 by Welbeck,
an imprint of Hachette Children's Group

10 9 8 7 6 5 4 3 2 1

Text copyright © Zaro Weil, 2025
Illustrations copyright © Junli Song, 2025

A CIP catalogue record for this book is available from the British Library.

ISBN 978 1 803 38153 4

Printed and bound in China

The paper and board used in this book are made from wood from responsible sources.

MIX
Paper | Supporting
responsible forestry
FSC® C104740
FSC
www.fsc.org

Welbeck
An imprint of Hachette Children's Group
Part of Hodder & Stoughton Limited
Carmelite House, 50 Victoria Embankment, London EC4Y 0DZ

An Hachette UK Company
www.hachette.co.uk

www.hachettechildrens.co.uk

The authorised representative in the EEA is Hachette Ireland,
8 Castlecourt Centre, Dublin 15, D15 XTP3, Ireland (email: info@hbgi.ie)

I HEAR THE TREES

UNTAMED POEMS
FROM MOTHER EARTH

Zaro Weil

illustrated by Junli Song

WELBECK
CHILDREN'S BOOKS

Contents

Contents

when I walk

wide-eyed

through today

yesterday is forgotten

tomorrow faraway

I HEAR THE TREES

I hear the trees
gather in sunbeams—
it is loud as all those
flutter-songs of
summer-end birds

I smell the orange

crinkle of leaves

spiralling through husky fall air—

feel the brushes of tiny beasts

burrowing inside swells of

rough bark

I watch autumn glow
through still warm trunks
then surge to earth
feeding a hungry spread of
root-tangles with enough light
to last through
deep winter and perhaps
the spring after that

it is now

I can't help but wonder as

I collect my own day—

have I gathered in enough

seen heard smelled

deep enough

to grow my own

memory-roots

enough to last until tomorrow

and perhaps

all my flutter-song springs

after that

I LOVE YOU

I love you says the bug to the moss

I love you says the moss to the rock

I love you says the rock to the mountain

I love you says the mountain to the sky

I love you says the sky to the sun

I love you says the sun to the moon

I love you says the moon to the sea

I love you says the sea to the Earth

As Earth says I love you to

Everyone

BAMBOOZLED BERRIES

the blossomest blossoms
the buddingest buds
burst from branches of the
brilliant bush

oh they were blue blue beauts

bunches of bounteous berries
brimming blazing bright balls
beneath a blowy bonanza of
balmy breezes but…

beware

babbling boldface birds
bemused by the bounty of the
beauteous bluey berries have a
brainstorm and billowing below in a
blaring blast of bombastic bird-banter
brazenly begin to
besiege the berries and
with a breathtaking big bold
beaky birdie binge get
busy busy busy
in a brisk blissful barrage of
bite bite bite

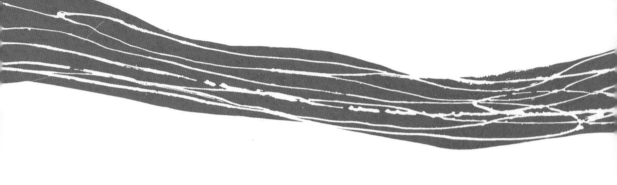

oh
bother bother bother
bemoan the bewildered

befuddled baffled bitten

bedraggled and thoroughly

bamboozled berries—

how balefully bleak

how bitterly beastly—

things would have been

bloomin' bloody better

by the blinkin' bunch

if only we had been born

bumpy brainy bits of

blah blah blah

bland old

boring old

broccoli

SPRING HULLABALOO

today
my two little dogs
unleashed from winter
charge all big barks up the
whisper-green hill
throw themselves onto
their backs and panting
kooky with love
go wiggling wild
side to side to side
rolling down the
velvet slope
which just happens to be
up-popping a
spring hullabaloo of
yellow-noisy
miniature…

daffodils

DROP

BY DROP

BY DROP

Orbiting bee in fresh buzzing garden

goes

Visiting flash new blooms

with

So many honeyed kisses

as

Pearly rain-beads land on quivering stems

while

Thirsty leaves unfurl gloss-green

and

Drop by drop by drop earth waits

until

Scents burst colour-mad from damp ground

when

Sun finally streams a chirpy new spring

into

Everyone's hungry petalled hearts

THREE NOISY FROGS

three green frogs singing

more frogs join croaking chorus

'out of tune' sobs moon

three flying bats squark

dozens more dive screeching loops

'pipe down' pleads poor moon

three plumed roosters crow

earth yawns flash-loud morning songs

moon fades

seeks quiet

THE STORY OF RUBY-WONDERFUL BEET

Beet sat very fat under earth

waiting for someone to move the turf.

Pull it out.

What in the world was taking so long?

Surely it was time to be picked.

Beet's once tiny clump of

underground seed clusters grew

knotty-round with worry…

and yet

there were certain things it was

well… certain of.

It knew spring had passed
because spotty green rain was no longer
splashing Beet's baby-breath shoots.

Then, as a gaggle of its
shine-happy leaves
strained to catch some yellow warm and
as Beet could feel a mob of
lightning-fast weightless creatures
make merry under its deepening roots…
it figured summer had rolled around.

So Beet

    waited

        and waited…

till rising on-the-move wind swirled

pillow-piles of autumn clouds

through the sky.

    Still Beet waited.

Of course, by now

every single earthworm had

burrowed down and coiled up into a

slime-coated ball…

for each had stopped wiggling about

hoping cold winter frost

would soon play itself out.

Naturally after all that
every other normal beet
found its way into someone's basket.
But not our brilliant Beet.

Fact was
Mother Earth had other things in mind.
She held on very tight.
So very tight that no one
    could possibly uproot her beet.

And now Beet could do nothing else but…
    well…
        keep on growing.

So it did just that.

It grew some more and then

even more until it fattened and bulged

this way and that…

till it was the biggest

    most different

        most brilliant

            ruby-wonderful beet that ever was!

'*Ah ha*' smiled Mother Earth

(who was very pleased with what she had pulled off).

Now that's exactly when

great big wondrous Mother Earth herself

laughed and laughed…

knowing full well that

everything

    she grows is completely different

      absolutely brilliant and

      always and forever

           earth-wonderful.

MORNING STILL

morning still

no clouds drift

no air stirs

just a small bird

shaking up the

quiet light

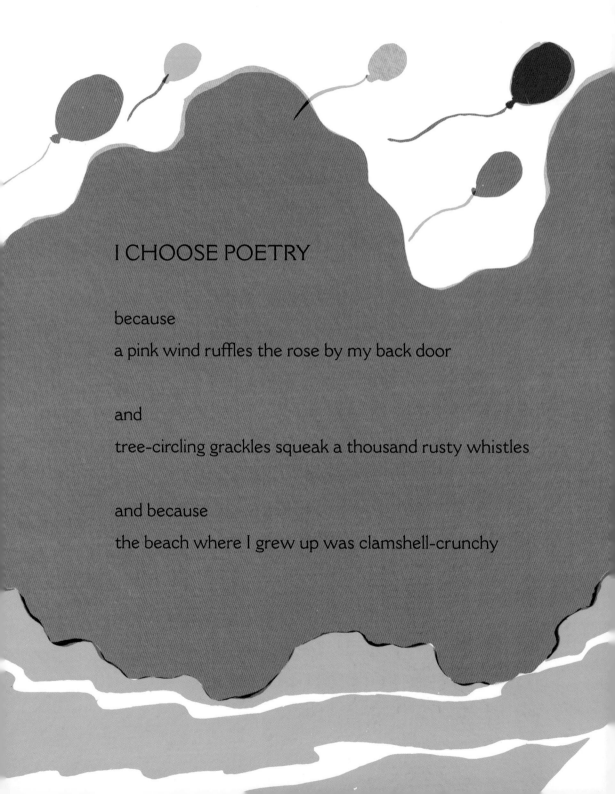

I CHOOSE POETRY

because
a pink wind ruffles the rose by my back door

and
tree-circling grackles squeak a thousand rusty whistles

and because
the beach where I grew up was clamshell-crunchy

and because

balloons flew wild at my sixth birthday party

and because

two snails stretch polished-fat on wet stones

and because

the sky spills its blue into the sea every summer

and because

clouds sometimes decide to sleep on my window

and because

lavender smells as big as purple sun

and because

my hug-happy dog Clementine died last year

and because

and because

all I want to do is tell someone about this

I need the best words I can find

so

I choose poetry

and

in writing these things down

I'm surprised for I

can't help but imagine—

poetry has chosen me

because

poetry is like that

poetry is personal

LADYBIRD HERE

Yooouuu hoooo!
Remember me?
Ladybird here!
I popped by to see you
Just this day last year.

What?   No?
Sure you don't remember me?
The bug with the perfectly perfect polka dots
Who tiptoed down your thumb
That afternoon when you turned one?

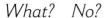

What? No?

Well… glad you're not asleep this year.

Because now that you're two

I can't help but notice

How much bigger your thumb grew!

HAPPY BIRTHDAY, FRIEND!

P.S. I'm off on a delicious tiny aphid hunt. Want to join?

What? No?

Oh. I understand. You prefer ice cream and cake.

LETTER TO A WORM
FROM A SWEET POTATO

hey worm

am I glad to see you
'cos here I sit
an orange-curious lump
peekaboo roots
     barely breathing in the
deep down
so blind-dark
heavy-heavy   of earth
stuck-stuck
when
whoop-whoop
     it all happens

I spot you and your

slither-slide army so

busy-busy digging

   quiver-tiny paths

      zigzagways routes

         squirm-brown roads

all around me so

I says to myself

this is my finest hour

'cos now my

    very-very own

pale-pale minuscule   roots

can finally spread their way

through

    the big underneath of

    the big everything

and find all the

heaven-food

they need to grow

which means worm

lickety-split

bing   bang   boom

I can turn into the

    lump-round

    orange-happy

     big fat sweet potato

I was always meant to be
　　　so
whoop-whoop again
I thank you　friend
　　and your whole
　　　　wiggle-wonderful
　　　　　　worm-squirmy army

OK　loads of
lumpy-bumpy love from your
sweetly-sweetly grateful
finally-finally
all　grown　up

orange-happy
sweet potato

43

MIDNIGHT BRIGHT

midnight bright

a dozen-and-one nightingales

can they hear

the full moon

RECIPE FOR A PERFECT
SPRING BIRTHDAY CAKE

1. Take a few deep breaths of almond blossom and shake
them into your palest green bowl trying not to spill.

2. Add two drops of new lavender clouds
(they must be soft enough).

3. Stir in one cup of big wind gusts and two cups
of pearly see-through downpours.

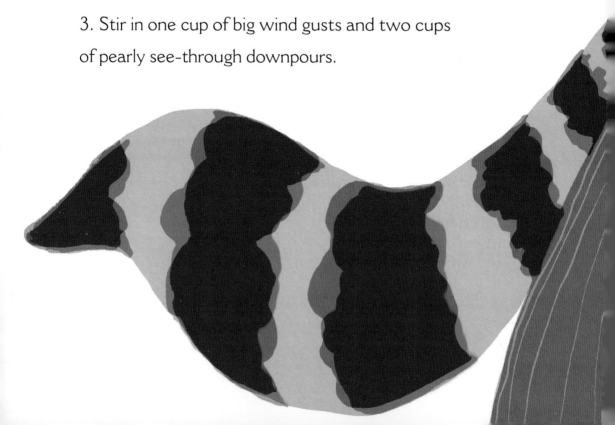

4. Combine eight tablespoons of white daisy petals with twenty-one teaspoons of oak leaf buds (you can also substitute dandelion puffs if desired… but the taste will be noticeably different). Shake well.

5. Mix in as many frog croaks as you can find as well as a big dash of tweets (cheerful chirpy ones probably work best).

6. Sift out a dozen pleasing wiggle-worms through fifty tablespoons of damp clotted earth. Add to bowl (depending on worm availability you might require either more or less earth).

7. Finely chop a few choice blades of un-mown grass for a more natural seasoning. Use as desired (cook's tip... I often add a few prickly brambles for texture at this step).

8. Let everything gently bake in a fresh sunbeam for a few weeks (possibly more if winter is acting stubborn).

9. Remove slowly (when there is no hint of a thunderstorm) and let sit until fully ripe.

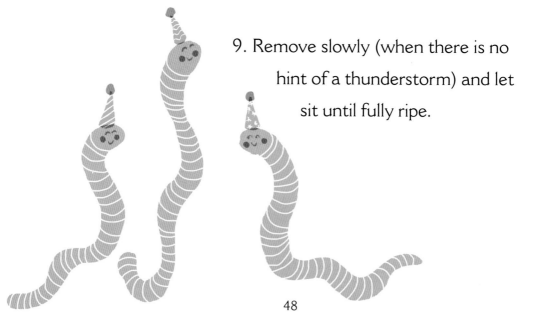

FOR THE ICING

Carefully choose the
tenderest roses you
can find and melt
their fragrance
onto your cake
moistening with
rain-bowed wildflower
mist. Then quickly drench
it all with a moon-mix of silver
sparkles adding some emerald-bright four leaf clover
sprinkles over everything for that final decorative garnish,
as well as for that special birthday pinch of good luck.

Blow up the balloons, light the candles,
invite your friends and serve at once.

P.S. Remember, there is no need to slice.

HOW DO THE FLOWERS DANCE

How do the flowers dance…

   in a joy-shake of dazzle and flutter-fun razzle

How do the clouds play…

   in a sky-game of puffs and frilly white ruffs

How does the sea sing…

   in a great swell of blues and rolling loud hues

How does the sun laugh…

   in a beam-load of grins and high-flying spins

How does the rain talk…

   in drizzled loud splashes and nonstop wet dashes

How does the comet sail…

   in a rush of gold glitters and silvery skitters

How does the fire think…

   in flames crackle-bright and hot-headed light

How do I dream…

   in make-it-up twirls and awesome mind-swirls

TYRANNO'S GREAT BIG HORRIBLE TALE

Wait a minute, little bird!
I have something very important
top secret
amazingly hush hush
to tell you.

Come on...
Don't hop away.
I can't hurt you.
This is important.
You have GOT to know,

WE ARE COUSINS!

Family Reunion

Hey! Come back, little bird!

I am serious.

I know you must feel scared but

you don't need to. Promise.

After all, now is now and NOT

66 million years ago when

I was 15 tons alive

huge, mean and completely

HORRIBLE.

Little bird,

if I had seen you back in those

earth-rumble times—

I would have opened my

steel-powerful jaws

gleamed my beastly

serrated-sharp teeth

risen from the fuming, smoking mud on

giant hind legs and

R O A R E D

till the ancient forests rattled and

shook down to the bottoms of their

cretaceous roots

and then

    and then

snaking my thick long neck in

drooling monstrous glee

madly SCARFED YOU DOWN in a wet shlurp…

    without

        thinking

            twice.

But, haha! Luckily for you
you weren't around then.
And like I said, now is now.

WAIT! STOP!

Fly on back here!
Don't be worried.

SEE the secret is—are you ready for this—
my direct cousin, Coelurosaurus,
had teeny, tiny microscopic

FEATHERS!!!

I mean, little bird,

they weren't fluffy like yours

but they were definitely little quill-things.

AND Coelurosaurus also had a

brain in the shape of

    —wait for it—

    a baby bird.

Can you believe that?

But it's TRUE! Ask anyone.

Come on! Stop quivering.

I'm coming to the good part.

Because, little bird, what happened is that

as the years rolled on

weirdly, oddly and curiously

Coelurosaurus grew littler.

Just imagine…

things usually grow

bigger!

But not your STRANGE cousin. It just got
smaller

    and smaller

        and smaller

   till

   it was a real live miniature of our

colossal dinosaur family.

Wait! Come on back!
Fluff into a nice feathered ball, bird.
You'll love this next part.

You see, sometime during the years
when Coelurosaurus was *tinifying*,
it began to grow bird-like feathers
then it began to flap its arm-wings
and

shazam

magic

va-voom

my cousin learned to fly
and then…

BOOM BOOM BOOM

It evolved into a you!

A little bird!

So YOU are a miniature relation of ME!

How about that!

Anyhow, just thought you'd want to know

After all, I have been your cousin for the past

66 million LONG years!!!!!

Sooooooo

You can go ahead and call me by my nickname

Tyranno (short for Tyrannosaurus rex)

Hey!

Hold your horses!

Don't take off without saying goodbye!

I promise not to…

Little bird…

Come back…

PLEASE come back…

I have another awesome true story…

See once there was this giant chunk of star called meteor that fell to earth…

WAIT! Don't fly off!

We are family…

And I'm not hungry…

Promise

PRETTY PLEASE LITTLE BIRD…

COME BACK…

HONEST!!!!

We could be FRIENDS!!!!!!!!

STRETCHING THE TWILIGHT

a long summer day
stretching the twilight
hundreds of swallows
circling diving

thousands of fat frogs
jumping croaking

millions of flashy fireflies
glittering dancing

as the hot moon rises

and every shadow
twining pulsing

summer-shorter

TEN MICE STAR IN A TINY POETICAL ADVENTURE

ten mice race outside
pink noses twitching for treats
eagle glides above

uh oh

ten mice dash to hide
scamper into tall grasses
eagle dives down fast

uh oh

ten mice hold their breath
not one little whisker moves
eagle confounded

uh oh

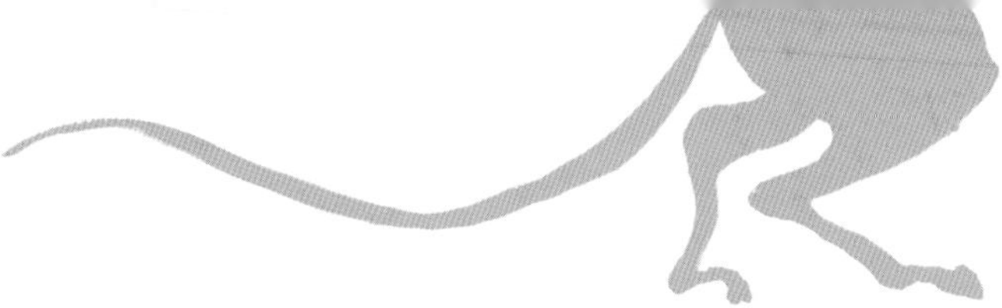

ten mice keep so still
eagle gets bored with those mice
swoops off to hunt hares

uh oh

ten mice scramble out
hungry after that big chase
but sniffing cat prowls

uh oh

ten mice shake in fear
hate that big cat-awful beast
take off very fast

uh oh

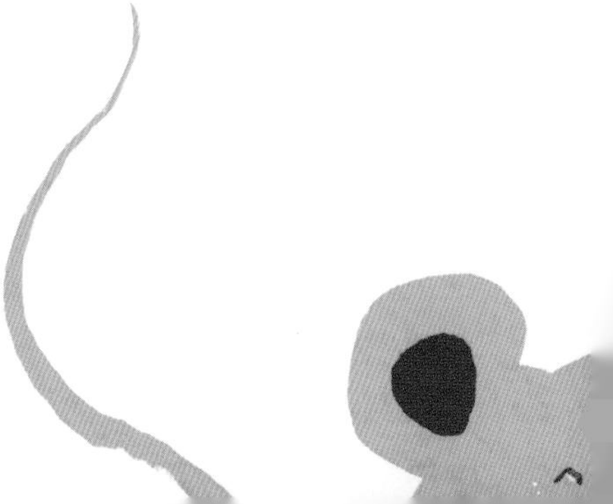

ten mice scurrying

cat tries to catch up and pounce

mice dart under bush

uh oh

ten mice giggling

it's a thorny berry bush

cat cannot reach them

oh ho

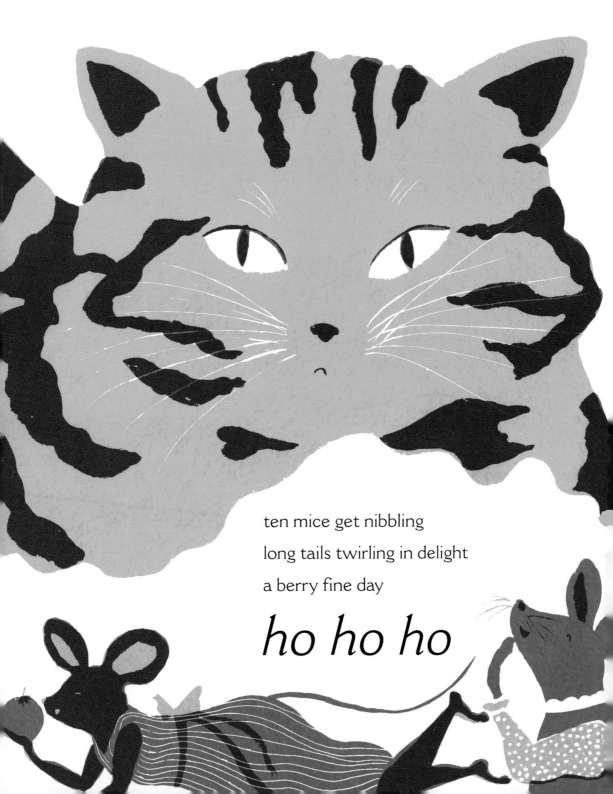

ten mice get nibbling

long tails twirling in delight

a berry fine day

ho ho ho

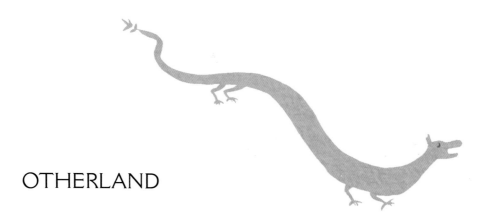

OTHERLAND

The last time I visited *Otherland*

Stars giggled out loud when trees bounced up and down

Clouds all joined puffs playing games with the sea

As fishes sang songs and danced next to me

Dragons read stories from books in the skies

While ants whistled rhymes munching fat poem-pies

Dogs barked long words wagging alphabet tails

Cats leapt over stars chasing rainbow-stripped whales

Elephants and hippos sipped tea on the moons

Which were bobbing and shining and

Attached to balloons

Flowers bloomed colours way under the earth

As funny-faced pumpkins told jokes with great mirth

Bats wove ripe star-shine into rivers of silk

And were helped by mosquitoes and bugs of that ilk

Raindrops flew upwards all night and all day

Passing gumdrops sweet-spinning every which way

Then grinning a thought as I headed to bed…

Otherland is fun

GOSH

I could live there instead

LETTER TO SPRING FROM WINTER

Dear Spring, my old friend,

Can't fool me!

I know you're there.
I heard you deep inside
that peach-puff cloud
this afternoon.

Then
when my last ice-breath
wind-spun towards earth yesterday—

I couldn't help but spot that
tiny blink of new snowdrop.
One of yours I think.
Haha, Spring!

And did I mention trees—
no longer wind-stabbing
skeletons
every branch now soft-outlined
decorating the distance in
shadows of just-green.

Or
how about those
slow-sail scents
twining madcap loops through
rose-flowered sky
flush with slip-slide
rain dots?

In fact, there's lots more
I could talk about—
your dizzying
insect-scuttles
colour-ruffles
sunbeam tangles.
Not to mention those
happy-go-lucky
warm wind-doodles!

However,
I think it's quite clear, Spring,
that whatever I do
no matter how hard I try
you will outwit me.
So I might as well
just… well…
give in and welcome you!

Only please remember,
old friend,

you may have your
heady way with earth now—
rushing melted snow into
giddy rivers and streams
flying pollen-pops helter-skelter
bursting blossoms day and night—

but tomorrow I will be back.

You see truth is, Spring

you need to remember—

in a few months

I'll take over again, while you—

you spend some quiet time alone.

Just imagine.

You can go curl up in the

faraway underneath of things and

start dreaming your riotous

mind-boggling moments of

new beginnings.

Love and shiver-snowy hugs,

Winter xxxxooo

CAT COULDN'T HELP IT

(Dedicated to Bob the Cat, forever
protector of Kew Bookshop…)

couldn't help it

there was something
OUT THERE
so dangerously mystifying
that he simply
could not stop or
break or interrupt his
green-eyed gaze—
he sat
fully sun-cuddled
—on guard—
in that particular
bookshop window

cat couldn't help it

nothing moved
not a hair on his head
not a whisker
ear tail or nose
nothing at all
except a thousand and one
sharp crescent-eyed gleams
darting straight through the
window-pane

hours passed
a long string of hours—
at last the sun yawned   and
clawing in what was left of her beams
stretched a solitary
sleep-dusted orange   before
curling tight into twilight

cat couldn't help it

he circled his head
snapped his eyes night-wide
and   lifting a paw coolly
licked off the day
in a single
flick of pink

settling back down into the
soft purr of evening—
with a sweep of
ginger-puffed rolls and
whisper-soft arches—
cat adjusted every bit
of himself   till he was
fully moon-cuddled

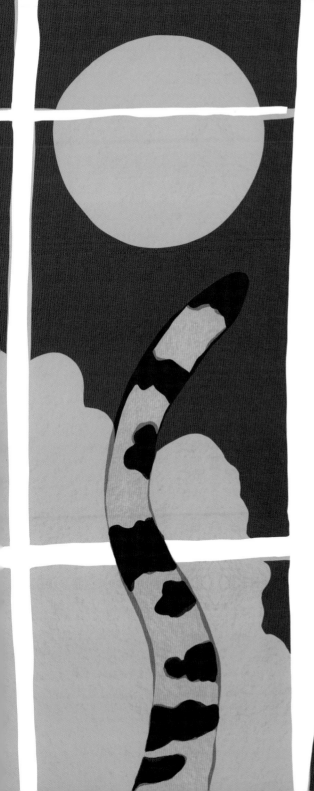

and only then
did he continue his…
green-eyed gaze
this time pin-prick
narrowing in on some
worrying dark shadows

cat couldn't help it

after all
cat was cat
insisting on protecting
day and night
every single book
in that particular
cat-loving
bookshop window

WOWIE-ZOWIE

wowie-zowie

tall tree

I love you

I gung-ho

ding-dong

ring-a-ling

love you—

more than any other

flim-flam

hurly-burly creature in the

whole round earth

giant universe or

razzle-dazzle cosmos

loves you—

after all tall tree

  nobody else thinks about

    mmmmmmmmmmmeeeeeeeeeeeeeeeee

  like you do

   nobody else tree that

   high high high very high up

    bothers to make it so

     easy-peasy for me to eat their

    hunky-dory leaves

    bobbly berries or

     tutti-fruitti treats

      during the sun-beamy day or

      moon-cheery night—

so thanks tippy-tall tree

see with you I don't have to

teeter-totter bend way over

to find bits of yums on the ground

instead

I'm super-duper

hip-hop cool and my

loosey-goosy long long neck

doesn't have to get so

wishy-washy tired going

flip-flop

whirly-twirl   so no matter how you

up and down   say it

up and down   spell it

up and down   think it

all the   I slap-happy

dilly-dally time—   fancy-free

tee-hee

silly-billy

LOVE YOU—

there

now everyone knows

TALL

GIRAFFE

LOVES

TALL  TREE

Ok bye for now

giraffe

P.S.

please don't worry tree

I would never ever nibble even one

lovey-dovey little heart  on your

topsy-tall

barky-beautiful

trunk

JUST SLEEPING

rusty brambles tangle stiff into autumn cool

as

scarlet-crisp leaves whirl inside rising pleats of wind chill

as

mushrooms shoot though piles of dark earth-crunch

as

bird flocks follow ancient sky paths to distant warm spots

as

six-legged creatures race to find hidden safe places

as

everything dream-waits for those bright-eyed new brambles

and

for every other just sleeping

spring thing

RAIN TODAY

rain today

cloud-heavy sky
water falling rope-thick

raging rivers
flood the window panes

branches sway
breathless in wind-mad gusts

mud soft-slides fast
over hard summer earth

birds all vanished
crickets escaped
bumpy toads hide under slippery
smooth rocks

and me

I sit quiet
drenched in slow smiles
holding my book close
all ready for today's
bright shiny story

MY BRILLIANT SHEEPDOG

My brilliant sheepdog
loves
playing frisbee.

The second I throw that
flat little disc through the woods
she squeals, yips and barks
like some ginger-wild beast—
    a four-legged, tail-waving
    ears-flying   dart of a dog
as every fluffed-up inch of her
charges after frisbee.

Because at such a rapturous
frisbee-in-the-air moment
nothing else in the world matters.
Only that little neon-bright
flying saucer.

Trees tremble with the thrill of it.
Sun does a double-take.
Wind laughs loopy gusts—
    everyone spell-bound
    by this high-speed
    winner-take-all race.

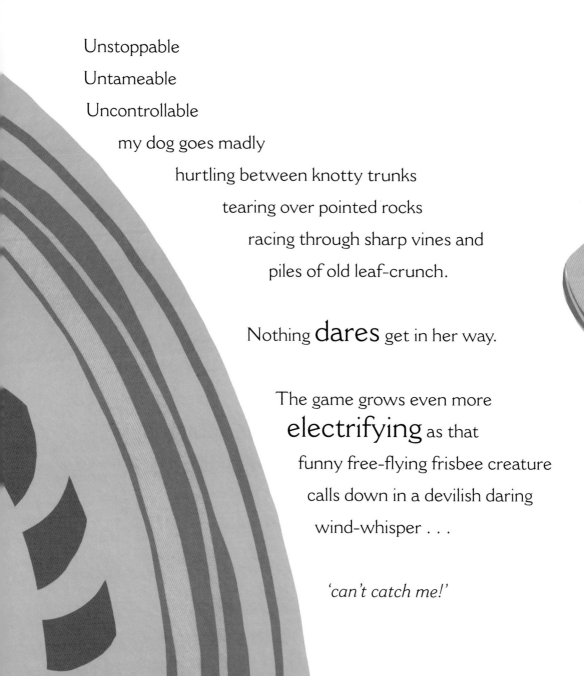

Unstoppable

Untameable

Uncontrollable

my dog goes madly

hurtling between knotty trunks

tearing over pointed rocks

racing through sharp vines and

piles of old leaf-crunch.

Nothing **dares** get in her way.

The game grows even more
electrifying as that

funny free-flying frisbee creature

calls down in a devilish daring

wind-whisper . . .

'can't catch me!'

It feels like an eternity of a race
until finally poor frisbee
out of breath and (at last)
    out of push
slow-rides a passing breeze
    back down to earth.

And THAT is when
my brilliant dog
in a dizzying bold leap
springs up and with a mouth-wide-open
snap
leaps to catch frisbee mid-landing.

Everything stops.

It's over.

Trees go back to calm slow-growing.
Sun continues its normal shine   while
wind laughs great big
that-was-fun-see-you-later   gusts.

But it's **not** over.
Clenching the disc tight between
sparkle-sharp teeth
my crazy pooch shakes frisbee
up and down… up and down
like she is teaching that
frisbee-creature
some kind of great   life   lesson

Fact is again—
Down deep inside her
clever doggy brain
my dog understands that

frisbee is really a

poor sheep in disguise—

    a sad little

    flat little

    misguided thing

who carelessly wandered off and

got lost in the big blue sky.

And of course only she   my

brilliant hero of a

brilliant sheepdog

can rescue poor lost frisbee-sheep.

Because that is exactly what sheepdogs

have been doing… well… forever!

And

way   way long before frisbees were

ever   ever   ever invented!

S H H H H H

sleep well   bud—
don't move an inch
just imagine a trillion
whipped-up wind trails
curling your soon-to-be
new scent
through a prism of
tinted sun speckles and
quicksilvered water dots

then
it might be fun to think about
who
out of a zillion creatures
is getting ready to soft-balance
its six improbable little legs

on your fattening petals
before dipping into all that
pollen dust swooning whisper-soft
soooo deep-sweet down
inside you

are you ready   bud
because in just a very few
parading moon crescents
sun orange drumbeats—
it will be your turn to open and
greet tomorrow
which has been waiting
just   for   you
a very long time

so shhhhhh

sleep well bud
things are about to get
a quintillion times
exciting

RAZZMATAZZ FUNGI

hidden in fields and forests
dwells a razzmatazz world of
wondrously weird fungi—
up-popping at night like
little curls and slices of
neon-coloured moons
right here on earth—
   fluorescent green streaks
   on dark branches
   gleaming purple knobs
   on rough bark
   shiny orange mini-saucers
   each so bejewelled and bright—

and   if
you should just happen to meet
a razzmatazz night fungi
and   if
you should just happen to
    put your ear very close—
you can just hear it
breathe your name in a
wondrously   weird   way

STOP PUSHING

please stop wind

I know you are the very biggest strongest thing
    on this Earth
but please stop pushing
everything   everywhere

slow   down   wind

just   think
    about me for a minute
what if my fresh-painted petals
get too shaggy and go
sailing away in one of your
winding whirligigs
far to the way-other-side
of the globe

and   then
what if one of my
new-born blooms
snaps off
        falls to the ground—
lying there broken-hearted
like a sad sad smudge
of ragtag pink dirt

look   wind
I know you are
strong as planet-twirl
big as measureless sky
lighter than any sunbeam-flick
because most days I can hear you
telling clouds where to go
giving raindrops their directions
stampeding dust
from one side of the world

to another—

you   see   wind

I know you have all the power to do

whatever you want

whenever you want

but   truth   is

if   I could see you in person

if   you could be solid for just a blink

right in front of me

I would tell you directly face to face

breath to breath

stop pushing

everything

everywhere

because a rose   wind

is also

no   small   thing

LISTEN STARS EARTH TALKING

listen stars

moon sun and everything that moves big

a new life—human—has come into our midst

>   choose to welcome it

make its path smooth so it can walk to the brow of my first hill

listen wind

clouds and rain and everything that circles round

a new life—human—has come into our midst

>   choose to welcome it

make its path smooth so it can run to the brow of my second hill

listen grasses

rivers lakes trees mountains and everything that

makes its home on me

a new life—human—has come into our midst

>   choose to welcome it

make its path smooth so it can leap to the brow of my third hill

listen birds

and all who fly in the air

a new life—human—has come into our midst

　　choose to welcome it

make its path smooth so it can soar to the brow of my fourth hill

listen animals

and all creatures who live in harmony with me

a new life—human—has come into our midst

　　choose to welcome it

make its path smooth so it can travel

far beyond all my hills

*adapted from a Native American Poem

WHERE DOES THE WHITE GO

when the snow melts
where does the white go

for I have seen it appear
without a word
poised in the very first glaze
of morning sky—

but it is not the same white

and I have seen it
rolling puffy roundabouts
through a
crowded cloud sky—

but it is not the same

and I have seen it

far away

a dream-bright moon wisp

in night sky—

but not the same

perhaps

white just waits

to burst into colours

deep inside earth

colours

big bold and wild as

a rainbow sky

HOWL

AIEEEEEEE AIEEEEEE
OUEEEEEE OUEEEEE
OUOUOUOU OUOUOUOU

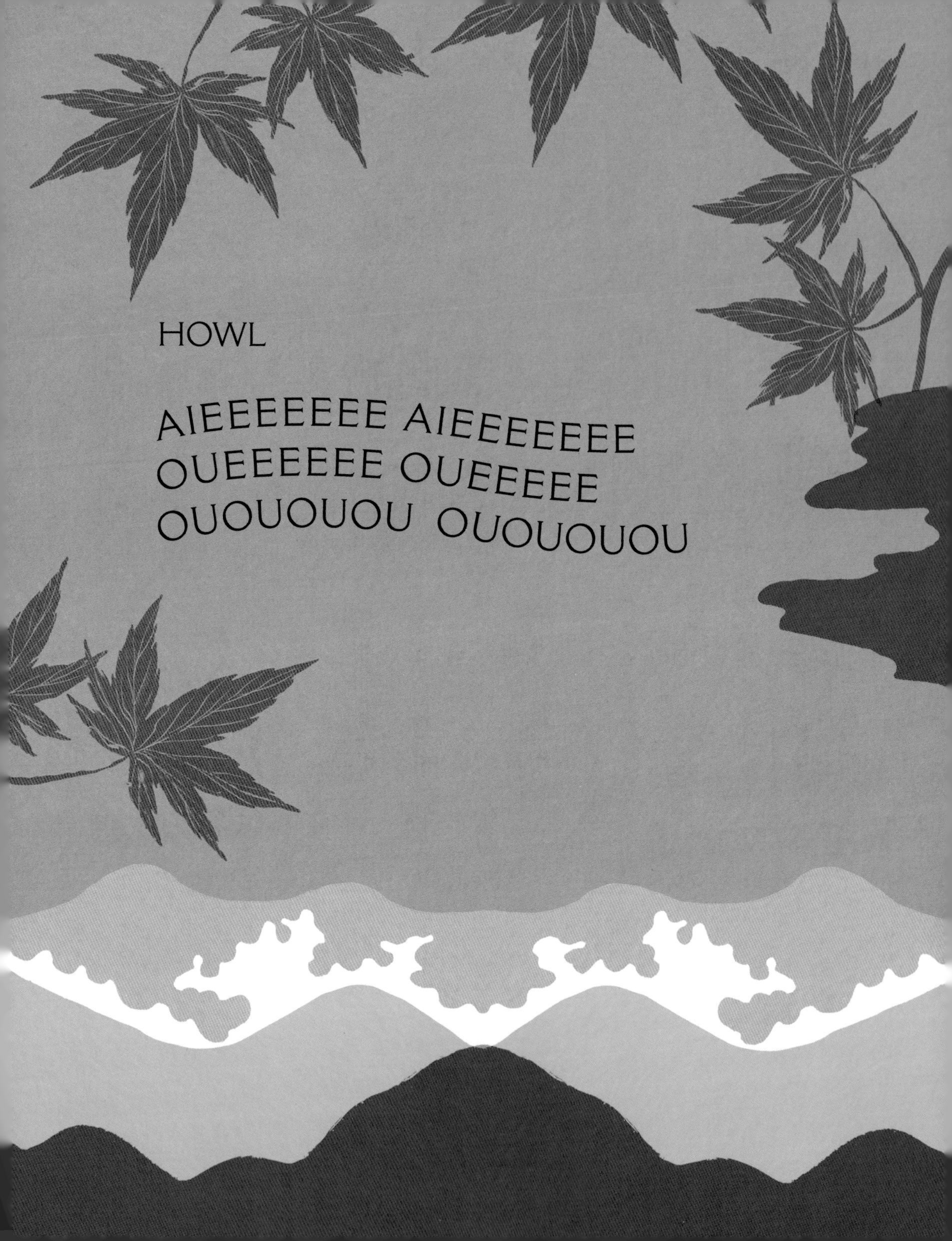

howl little cub

howl

don't hold back

flash those polished

amber eyes of yours

howl the scent of long ago

and if I teach you anything
know this new-found voice of yours
calls forth the great untamed

so when you want sun to rise
night to ignite its silent sparks
clear water to swell the river
howl
and when you stand
stiff-legged and tall
proud ears alert
teeth sharp-shined
confronting your prey
howl

of course when you must fly
escaping the bear
howl fierce
for earth to rise up fast
to meet your lengthening legs

then howl soft

when first you meet your

grey-furred partner

under a moon-flood of trees

on a trail of sweet shadows

and howl long

when you smell that blue of

berries growing darkly wild

outside your very own den

last thing little cub

when your mother is no longer

hunting beside you

howl full

your big wolf heart

for me

AIEEEEEE AIEEEEEE
OUEEEEEE OUEEEEE
OUOUOUOU OUOUOUOU

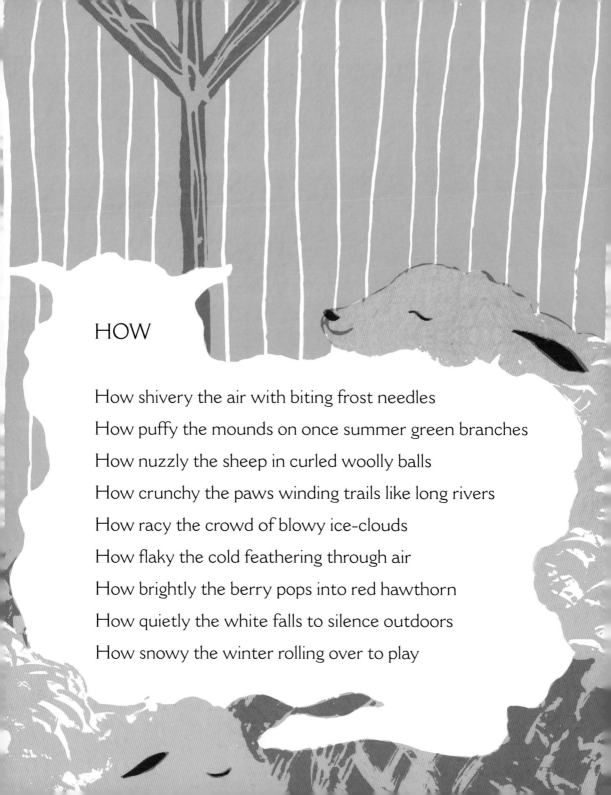

HOW

How shivery the air with biting frost needles

How puffy the mounds on once summer green branches

How nuzzly the sheep in curled woolly balls

How crunchy the paws winding trails like long rivers

How racy the crowd of blowy ice-clouds

How flaky the cold feathering through air

How brightly the berry pops into red hawthorn

How quietly the white falls to silence outdoors

How snowy the winter rolling over to play

BIG LOVE

Sung by a very old tree to a sapling

listen tree child

oh
I remember
bright sun
new light
cold rain
water so busy
sky so busy
downpour
downpour

listen tree child

118

oh

how beautiful it was

such power

earth grew strong

I grew strong

new roots

fat trunk

long arms

green song

green song

listen tree child

oh

it was good

my world

my forest

my friends

oh

I remember

tree child

such a time of

big earth love

big sky love

MY ANCESTORS

my ancestors would have
smelled this same earth
walked the same paths
seen the same flowers
sky sun stars

my ancestors would have
felt the same wind
chased the same rabbits
heard the same birds
frogs cats dogs

they would have

laughed the same laughs

swum the same waters

climbed the same mountains

rocks   cliffs   hills

but now

things are different

and I know

my ancestors would have

seen the same ruin

sighed the same sighs

cried the same tears

along with me

ALL TOGETHER ALL AT ONCE

now and then
when a timeless twilight
rolls over earth
flocks of high-sailing
starlings
all together
all at once
swell
into wind-stirring drifts of
shifting sky shapes
like some dark-surging
celestial beast
murmuring
startling
fragments
of
eternity

FUN IN FOUR SEASONS

When butterfly soars
sun opens its petalled heart
spring bird sings worm-fat

Just because they can
candy floss flowers bright-burst
summer commotion

Flying crinkle-leaves
helter-skelter earth creatures
autumn on the move

Fluffy winter flakes
fleece-white mounds cushioning earth
sheep laughing in snow

I SPOT IT

I spot it

through my night window

Floating

silent stripes between branches of the green oak tree

Playing

shadow games with silky leaf silhouettes

Cradling

feather-round robins tight-asleep in midnight nests

Lighting

paths for hungry mobs of scurry-fast insects

Sparkling

mosses and lichens busy soft-hugging rough bark

And it's now that I know...

Something special

shines on me too as I lie not quite sleeping

Wrapping

me in warm wavy shadows of

Moon's

big-hearted beams

DIRECTIONS TO THE NEXT UNIVERSE

1. Find a good seat in your *Starship* and fire each *Rocket* in the correct sequence towards the *Milky Way*, making sure to avoid dizzying *Pulsars* and troublesome grains of *Cosmic Dust*.

2. Follow the very next cloud of *Nebula* to the *Inner Planets* which are within the *Asteroid Belt* (*Mercury… Venus… Mars*).

3. From there take an *Elliptical Orbit* to the *Outer Planets* (*Jupiter… Saturn… Uranus… Neptune*). Don't be fooled by the many slow-turning *Satellites* launched from a multitude of global earth stations. They are not real stars.

4. Now carefully navigate your way through great swathes of real *Shooting Stars* (you might want to stop occasionally for a photo as bright-burning *Meteorites* fall like dazzling fireworks into earth's atmosphere).

5. When you eventually arrive at the dark *Kuiper Belt*, remember to dress up warm and then thoughtfully steer your craft through the thousands of wild-flying *Comets*, *Asteroids* and various bits of *Space Junk*.

6. Take a short break if you wish at one of the many *Star Constellations*. Following the directions provided, adjust your instruments to chart the next step which will take you safely past a sea of great *Black Hole Quasars*.

(Be extremely diligent during this phase. The last thing in the world you would want is to tumble into one of these hungry holes that lead to nowhere and where you would be trapped for a very long time. Forever, in fact).

7. It is only now that you can relax a bit as you find yourself floating through numerous *Starbursts* in new *Galaxies*. Of course, if you glance back through the rear window, it will become apparent that your home, *Planet Earth*, with its great blue and white swirls, is *Light Years* away. You might enjoy watching its slow rotation. And if you are extremely observant, you will also see its moon (the familiar one you see most nights) travelling its very own special orbit around *Earth*.

8. At this point, if cosmic luck is on your side, you might even hurtle past a fabulous *Supernova* exploding in a luminous *Stellar* bang.

9. At last you will arrive at the *Andromeda Galaxy* which is only 2.2 million *Light years* from Earth. It is so bright here that probably your family and friends might be able to spot you (even without a *Telescope*) and perhaps wave.

10. If you decide to continue, you must adjust all instruments to guide you safely to the next spiralling *Triangulum Galaxy*.

11. Of course, if you wish to return to your mother *Planet* at this stage, you could definitely be there for dinner. Just rotate your *Time Belt*, adjust your *Coordinates* to Earth and set your *Wavelengths* correctly.

12. When you are ready to time-space travel, remember to tap the *Quark-Star* which will ignite all the *Nuclear Particles* you require for a safe flight home.

13. Finally. Should you wish to return to continue your *Galactic* explorations tomorrow or even the day after, it is always possible to ask a passing *Astronaut* for a lift. But you must take care to make sure your *Anti-Gravitational Power* is fully activated and switched on.

Hope you have a very pleasant and exciting flight!

Please feel free to *Like* this travel site. We already have an astronomical number of *Likes*, and your *Like* could make all the difference.

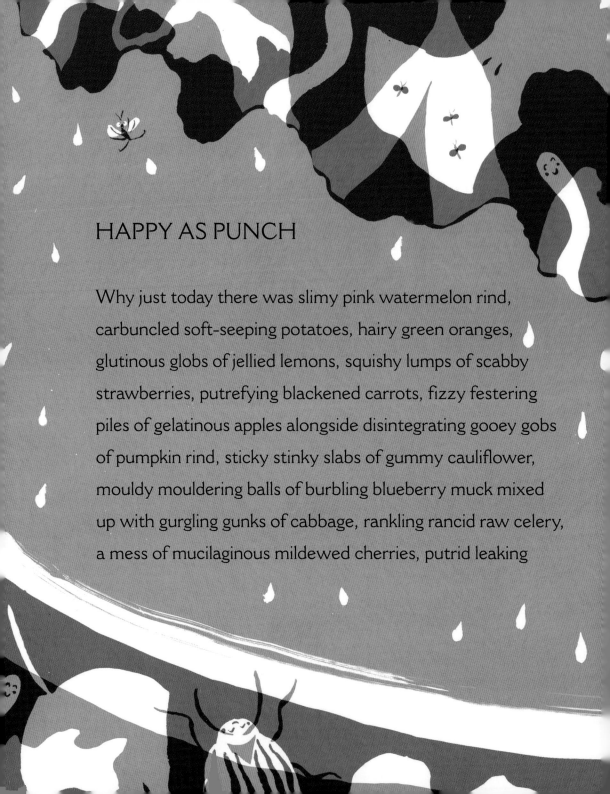

HAPPY AS PUNCH

Why just today there was slimy pink watermelon rind,
carbuncled soft-seeping potatoes, hairy green oranges,
glutinous globs of jellied lemons, squishy lumps of scabby
strawberries, putrefying blackened carrots, fizzy festering
piles of gelatinous apples alongside disintegrating gooey gobs
of pumpkin rind, sticky stinky slabs of gummy cauliflower,
mouldy mouldering balls of burbling blueberry muck mixed
up with gurgling gunks of cabbage, rankling rancid raw celery,
a mess of mucilaginous mildewed cherries, putrid leaking

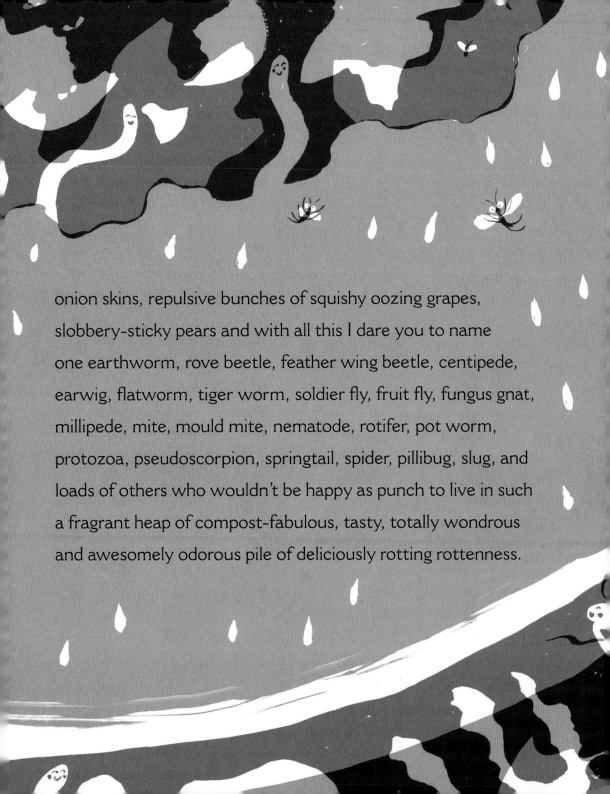

onion skins, repulsive bunches of squishy oozing grapes, slobbery-sticky pears and with all this I dare you to name one earthworm, rove beetle, feather wing beetle, centipede, earwig, flatworm, tiger worm, soldier fly, fruit fly, fungus gnat, millipede, mite, mould mite, nematode, rotifer, pot worm, protozoa, pseudoscorpion, springtail, spider, pillibug, slug, and loads of others who wouldn't be happy as punch to live in such a fragrant heap of compost-fabulous, tasty, totally wondrous and awesomely odorous pile of deliciously rotting rottenness.

STRAY DOG

walking alone
near the briny rocks
    —a visitor by the sea—
a stray dog followed me

I saw him avoiding a parade of
dust-loud trucks and
high-shined cars as
I crossed the street

    he must have heard me
    wishing for his safety

his fur was ocean-choppy

patched with pale scars

his thin frame a story of

hungry days

too-long-on-the-street

but his eyes were mild as

fresh foam and

warm with deep

circles underneath

as I walked

he stayed by my side and even

the bloated trash cans

dotting the sidewalk with

juicy scents

didn't stop him leaving me

I could tell

people passing by in

flip-flop sandals and

flash neon trainers

eating sticky popcorn and

rainbow mounds of candy floss

thought he was my dog—

they smiled

we were both proud

I wanted to give him food

soft toys and a bed

teach him to play ball

on the sand and

chase sticks into the water

but when I got to my door
he vanished—
rushing off
like a summer wave rolling
home

maybe he knew that
it wouldn't work out

I think he must have
attached himself to another
stranger
walking alone by the sea

someone
who might be around
tomorrow

BORED WITH WITCHES, GHOSTS AND GOBLINS

Late October.

Usual time. In bed.

Thinking about Halloween.

Figuring out my costume.

Because I am definitely

Bored with witches, ghosts and goblins.

Fed up with dragons, monsters and skeletons.

And everyone is a super hero something.

Not me.

I want to dress up as something unusual.

One of a kind.

Everyday. Yet astonishing.

Astonishing. Yet everyday.

A totally magical costume.

I stare out the window.

Blue sky folds away for the night.

Moon wisp turns up.

Cloud feathers on the move.

When an idea lights up inside!

The big outside.

I will be something from the big outside.

But what?

Where to begin?

OK. Creatures!

A bird?

A racing squirrel?

No. Too ordinary.

A worm. Ummm. Too wiggly.

A rabbit. Too jumpy.

A horse. Too fast.

A fish. Too slippery.

A porcupine. Too prickly.

A chicken. Too clucky.

A lion. Too bossy.

A unicorn. Too popular.

A frog. Too green and noisy.

A cat. Too stuck up.

A dog. Too many wags.

A spider. Too many legs

Maybe a plant!

A bush. Too boring.

A flower. Too many to choose from.

A tree. Too many branches.

A weed. Too stubborn.

A pumpkin. Too obvious.

A string bean. Too ridiculous.

Could be a big thing!

A mountain. Too still.

A river. Too wandering.

An ocean. Too salty.

A mud puddle. Too hard to guess.

A gust of wind. Too hard to see.

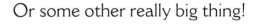

Or some other really big thing!

A cloud. Too changeable.

A raindrop. Too splashy.

A moonbeam. Too silvery.

A sun ray. Too hot.

A star shine. Too twinkly.

A rainbow. Too hard to find.

My eyes start to close.

Dream-swirls roll over my pillow.

Last gaze out the window.

143

Flash. Dazzle. Wow.

The sky!
It glows red-orange!
It dazzles yellow-gold!
It explodes peach-pink!
It flashes purple-violet!

It is perfect!

And in a gasp, two eye-pops and twenty big smiles,
I know. It's obvious.

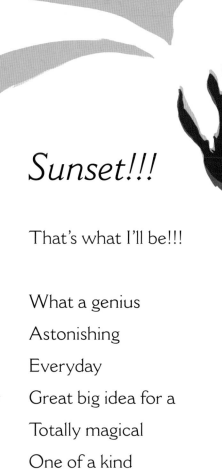

Sunset!!!

That's what I'll be!!!

What a genius

Astonishing

Everyday

Great big idea for a

Totally magical

One of a kind

Halloween costume!

P.S. I'm sure Mum won't mind making it!

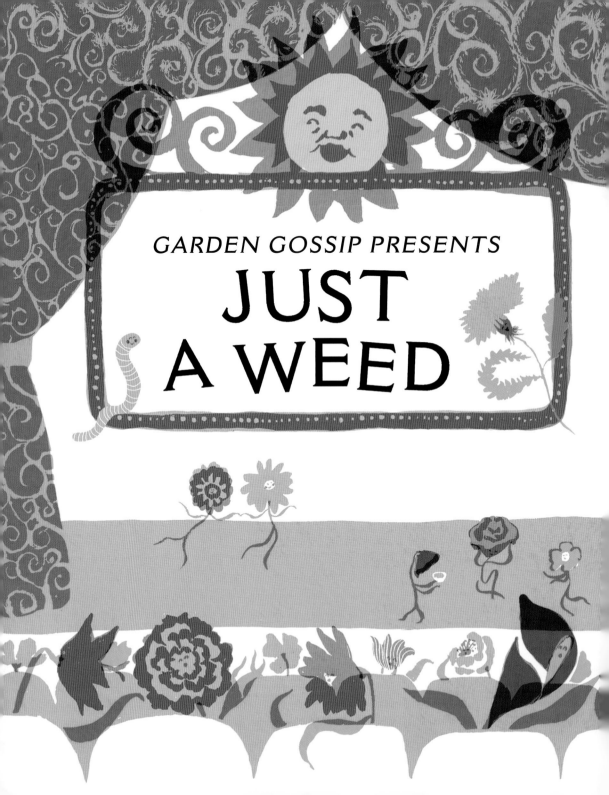

GARDEN GOSSIP PRESENTS

JUST
A WEED

A Little
Kew Gardens Play

WORM

Hey, Zinnia.

What's up?

Did you catch the size of your

neighbour this morning?

—

ZINNIA

Hey, Worm. I sure did.
Shocking! How could that
rapscallion of a dandelion
grow so much bigger than
me overnight! After all,
Worm, it's just a weed...
Hey, Daisy. Did you see
that invader of a weed
this morning in our
incredible garden?

—

148

DAISY

Did I ever! That yellow joker
dandelion is brighter than me
now and it's just a weed...
Hey, Rose, have you noticed that
giant ruffian in our great garden?

—

ROSE

Of course! That hooligan dandelion
doesn't belong anywhere near our
awesome garden. It is not, by any
stretch of botanical imagination, as
beautiful as me. Or even the rest of
you. It's just a worthless, deplorable,
detestable and positively dreadful
weed... Hey, Marigold, you always
look so smart and well-turned out
with all those perfect gold petals.
What do you think?

—

MARIGOLD

Thinking hard

Hey, everyone. I think we
need to talk to Dandelion.

—

ALL FLOWERS

Are you crazy, Marigold? Have you gone
mad in the sun? It's just an unpleasant,
doesn't-belong-here trespasser of a weed.
And right in the middle of our glorious,
gorgeous garden! The nerve!

—

MARIGOLD

Hang on! Just think about it.
Wouldn't you like to grow as fast
and big and strong as Dandelion?

—

ALL FLOWERS

Looking a bit sheepish

I suppose so.

—

They all turn towards Dandelion

—

Hey, Dandelion. We don't want you in our garden.

You're just a good-for-nothing weed.

But we do want to know how you grow so big. So tall.

So fast. How do you do it? What's your secret?

—

DANDELION

Hey, flowers. Don't complain.

You need me here.

Weeds are wonderful!

—

ALL FLOWERS

Haha. Says who?

—

DANDELION

Says me. Don't be so stuck-up. Listen and learn, flowers.

It's like this. My big secret is... I have super-power long roots

so I can dig way far down (with Worm's help) and make sure

that the earth is rich and happy and filled with fantastic food.

Which we all need! Right? Because as neighbours… my earth is your earth. See what I mean? Plus, and this is a big plus, insects like me a lot. And the more insects in the garden, the better for your pollination. So you can grow more of you. See what I mean? Another thing is that those insects then eat up other unpleasant little beasties that bother me. And that bother you, too! See what I mean?

—

ALL FLOWERS

Acting a bit nicer to Dandelion

We definitely see what you mean. Maybe you are right, Dandelion. Tall? Strong? Long roots? Great food? Insects eating bothersome beasties? Hmmmm. Not a bad idea. In fact, a galloping genius idea! OK, Dandelion, how do we get to be like you?

—

DANDELION

HA! Thought you'd never ask. Right. First things first. Hey, Worm. Think you could help out?

—

WORM

Sure! My buddies and I can clear lots of beautiful root space in earth for every flower. So they can dig deeper and get all the scrumptious food they need to grow.

—

DANDELION

Excellent suggestion, Worm. Good start. But, hey! Just had an incredible, out-of-sight and totally brilliant thought, Flowers! Why don't I invite my grow-like-lightning weed friends; Buttercup, Crabgrass, Purslane, Creeping Charlie, Nut Grass, Chickweed, Quack Grass, White clover, Shepherd's Purse and Canada Thistle. They would love to come here and help out. I mean, let's be honest. This is one heck of a scrumptious garden. And my weed pals would feel super showy proud here.

—

ALL FLOWERS

WHAT? Are you kidding? No thanks! A great big NO THANKS! That would be ten weeds too many. This is THE ROYAL BOTANIC GARDENS, KEW after all.

And let's get this straight, *flowers* and fabulous *trees* and *plants* rule. Not *weeds!* The only exception is just you! Anyway, big thanks, Dandelion for your help about roots and things. And thanks, Worm for your earth help!

—

ZINNIA

Okey dokey. We are ready! Let's get this garden growing. Perk up everyone! Visitors today! Gotta look GREAT! Stretch those stems. Get those blossoms shine-happy. Smile everyone! Say! Here's a super-duper great idea, Dandelion. Just thought of it. How about a race?

—

DANDELION

Hey, Zinnia. Super. I'm totally up for a good race. Let's do it! (This will be soooooo easy to win)! OK. Ready everyone?

—

Last one to reach the sky over KEW GARDENS is a rotten egg!

THE SOFTEST FALL IN THE WORLD

tulips never fade away
when it's time to say goodbye—
never get withered leaves
crinkled brown petals or
soggy stems

no
at the end tulips

tulips don't shrivel up   just keep sweet-talking—
lose their colours   each flower opening
droop their heads and go limp   ever wide   ever big
over the edge of the vase   stretching as far as it can
until it colour-gleams so thin
so see-right-through-other-worldly
that when it's finally that time to
let go of life—

petals simply drift off in the
softest fall in the world

and me

well

I can't help but wonder

as I hug my soft

very best friend of a

very old dog named Spot

when it's his turn to say goodbye

let go of life—

will he keep sweet-talking

until he drifts off

I think maybe he will—

but I know for sure

whatever happens

wherever he goes

he will always be right here

sweet-talking softly

inside me

THE WILD OF YOU

moon

what a ball of

odd possibilities

you are

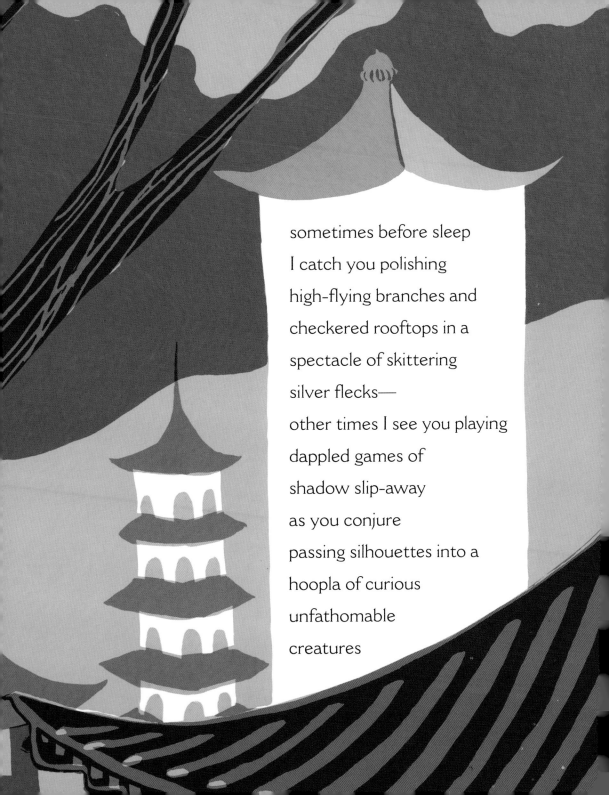

sometimes before sleep
I catch you polishing
high-flying branches and
checkered rooftops in a
spectacle of skittering
silver flecks—
other times I see you playing
dappled games of
shadow slip-away
as you conjure
passing silhouettes into a
hoopla of curious
unfathomable
creatures

then

when I'm by the sea

you often turn up

night-fractured

looking like a starry circus of

little tinsel-rounds

bouncing on the water

riding high

spinning choppy-wild

on top of every

ripple and roll

of course

once in a while

you fatten into a great

orange glow-ball and go

rolling off towards the thin

edge of the sky

and don't forget moon

those nights when you turn on

your fat waxing light so bright

that even sleeping buds

mysteriously burst open

all colourful triumph

thanks to you

while sweet sap races up

trunks   stems   stalks

seeking for some enchanted reason

your ancient sky-high

moon kingdom

until finally moon

that very big moment

once a month

when you are swollen so

perfectly round with shine

that the

strangest   things   happen—

oceans surge

tides rise higher

ebb lower and

all us creatures

we can't help but

howl   because it seems

yelp   everything

run circles   on the planet has some

fly frenzies   cosmic yearning for

lay eggs   the light of you

chant spells   the wild of you

bellow berserk   and all those

go a bit mad   odd

                        possibilities

                        you bring us here

                        on Earth

IF YOU CAME THIS WAY

if you came this way

you would see me

gliding easy in a school of friends

through water

exploring everything wet and smooth

there is to know—

something you can never

really understand—

perfect in my slippery world

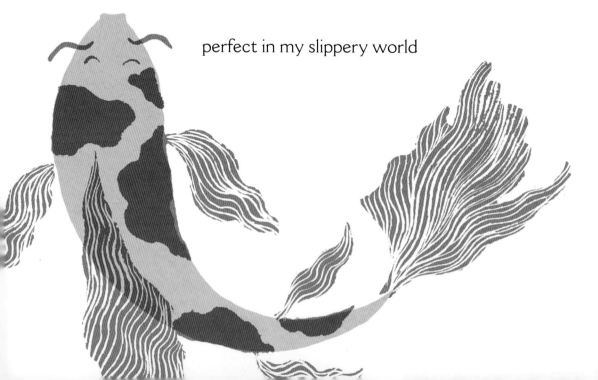

if you came this way
you would see me
jumping high-springing games
my curious big feet leaping boundless
as I race with my mob
exploring the thrill of almost flight—
something you can never
really understand—

perfect in my hip-hop world

if you came this way

you would see me

line-marching with buddies

collecting what I can carry

building bewildering stations

far underground

exploring the life of doing everything

all together—

something you can never

really understand—

perfect in my million-mates world

if you came this way
you would see me
a winged sun-sparkle
flying tiny circle-tints
exploring the fun of free—
something you can never
really understand—

perfect in my loop-the-loop world

if you came this way
if you came this way
perhaps
you might begin to understand
we are all
all of us here
perfect
in our
perfect worlds

IMAGINE

Imagine a dynasty that rules Earth

A universe of magical creatures

Right under our noses

Pulsing with primeval colours

In shades so preposterously painted

We cannot begin to name them all

Imagine a dynasty of infinitesimal forms

Outrageous and practical

So cockamamie weird and fantastical

We cannot begin to conjure them all

Such a colossal realm of

Alien-like creatures with

Far-reaching powers who forever

Feed protect inspire us—

An empire of triumphant earth-movers and

Six-legged shapers—

    Flyers, runners, crawlers, hoppers

    Creepers, shufflers, jumpers, wigglers

Whose quizzical antennae probe

Earth's deepest secrets—

One minuscule move at a time

Running the world we think

We know so well—

And this mighty dynasty

    Trilling, chirping, lisping, clicking

    Buzzing, squeaking, whining, zitting

This spellbinding realm of lilliputian beasts—

    Ten quintillion on-the-go wonder-workers—

More numerous than all

The grains of sand covering all the world

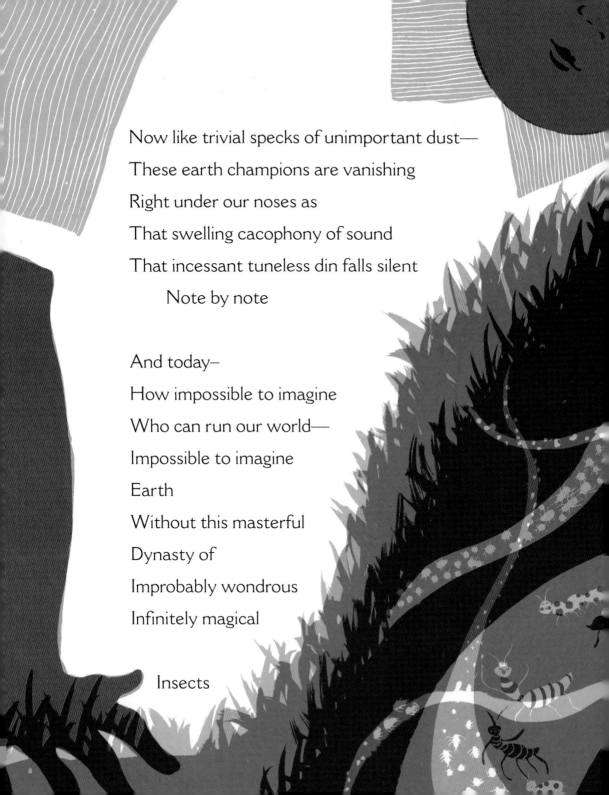

Now like trivial specks of unimportant dust—
These earth champions are vanishing
Right under our noses as
That swelling cacophony of sound
That incessant tuneless din falls silent
    Note by note

And today–
How impossible to imagine
Who can run our world—
Impossible to imagine
Earth
Without this masterful
Dynasty of
Improbably wondrous
Infinitely magical

Insects

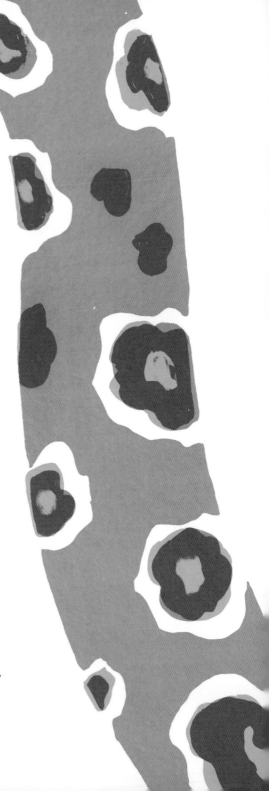

I SAW THE SNAKE

I saw the snake

that's a lie

I didn't see it
but my big sister did

the snake was in the garage
coiling delicate determined and
oh so double-quick between
bulging piles of bubblewrap…
sitting puffy-happy stuffed
shimmer-shiny-fat
proudly wrapping our
household yesterdays—
    favourite broken toys
    books too good to give away

and everything else

can't-throw-outable

of course

when she saw it she screamed

(*who wouldn't have screamed*)

it was big

(*seriously incredibly fearfully enormous*)

two metres at least

thick in dark grey stripes

she turned to run but

caught her dress —

a red, white and blue

broken old whirligig

(*one of Mum's can't-throw-outables*)

perched on a bottom shelf

snagged it

naturally my big sister's pulse

raced faster than a clock gone bananas —

she was sure the reptile had

risen up

clicking and hissing in a

snaky-tongue-flicking

corkscrew of a coil

grabbed her hem and

was about to strike

a dreaded

gruesome

hair-raising

poison-fanged

b   i   t   e

but the truth was

snake hadn't grabbed anything —

(*Dad was quite sure*)

it just wanted water

maybe a mouse and

a super good game of *pop the bubbles*

(after all you never can tell what tickles a snake Mum says)

and just maybe

(very probably in everyone's opinion)

this big thick snake really

had its heart set on a

sumptuous

serpenty

long summer

s t r e t c h...

a curlicue

whishing

spiralling

undulating

whirly-twirl

big game of fun

all over our family's

(absolutely we all agree)

can't-throw-outable

yesterdays

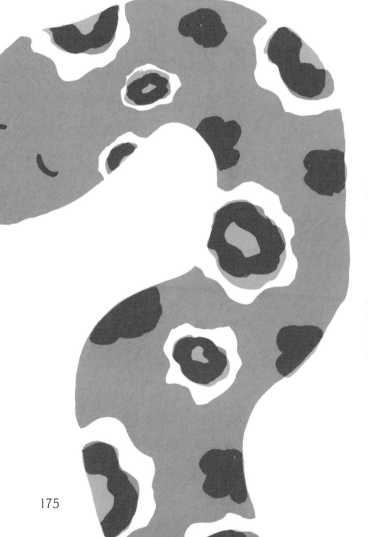

I TRIED TO CLAIM
THE MOUNTAIN

I tried to claim the mountain
thought it was mine
after all
I watched it every day —
saw how it woke up inside
a haloed mass of pale morning clouds
and how it sat at noon
wrapped silent in great stripes —
green now grey now green again

I noticed when it changed at twilight
into a frothy crimsoned peak
before finally sliding into deep night and
the purpled netherworld

daily nightly
I watched the mountain

smiled

as it sliced wind into strands

laughed

as it parted moon and sun into beams

but the mountain

didn't hear when I called out

didn't answer me at all

never noticed me

that is

I didn't think so

until one day

I felt a shattering of light

jarring of stone

storm of dust

as the mountain welled up inside

my wildest dreams and without

one word or rumbling breath

simply smiled back

and claimed me

WHAT DOES OWL SEE

what does owl see
with those yellow-gleam eyes
staring so sharp into far away—
past that dark night time everything
past that horizon of mystery-moons
    universe of star shines
    great milky way twirls

maybe owl spies seamless wind trails
streaming on forever in a
sky of effortless swoops—
    free-soaring dives
    never-ending flight
or maybe
owl observes faraway earth spots
where

creatures like us

  like you and me

  rest

our eyes stretched past the horizon towards

  a secret

  lit up

  deep-inside place

where mystery soars free in our thoughts

and

the universe gleams in our hearts

hold on tight to your world

for your world is my world

your planet my planet

Exploring some of the poems in more depth

This book is a perfect invitation for adults and children to talk about and engage in understanding the world, language and poetry together. Here are some ideas for how to explore some of the poems together in fun and engaging ways, provided by the Centre for Literacy in Primary Education; an independent charity that works with primary schools around the country and beyond to support them in developing best practice in all aspects of literacy teaching.

CLPE

CENTRE FOR **LITERACY**
IN PRIMARY EDUCATION

....

I HEAR THE TREES:

Read and talk about the poem:
Read the poem out loud together and discuss your initial impressions. *What did it make you think about? How did it make you feel? What made you feel this way? What words and phrases stay in your mind after reading? Why do you think this is?* Consider the title, **I Hear the Trees**. *What does this mean to you? What sounds might you hear if you listened to the trees? Why do trees 'gather in sunbeams'? Do you think you would really be able to hear this?* Now, re-read the poem, considering what is described in each verse. *What happens to the trees in different seasons? How do they support other life forms in their habitat? What helps them to survive through the changes in the seasons?* Re-read and think about the last part of the poem. *How are our needs as people similar to the needs of trees? What needs might we have that the trees might not? What helps us to grow strong and healthily? What supports our minds as well as our bodies?*

Explore the concepts:
Think again about all of the things you heard about in the poem. *Why are trees important to our planet? How do trees grow? What do trees need in order to survive? What do you think **we** can do to help them?* Find a seed from something which could be planted to grow into a tree. This might include an apple, orange or pear pip, acorns, sycamore, sweet chestnut or hazelnut. You'll also need a plant pot with drainage holes in the base, some small stones and compost. Put some stones at the bottom of the pot and fill it almost to the top with compost. Plant your seed into the pot of compost, about 2cm deep, then press down the compost and water it thoroughly. Check it every week to make sure the soil hasn't dried out. Be careful

not to over-water it. As the seed starts to sprout, keep an eye on the growth. Re-pot the shoot into larger pots as it grows. Once it reaches 40cm, find a suitable place to transfer it into the ground outside. Think about where you're planting in relation to your house, your neighbours, and any other buildings and make sure you have permission to plant on the land. You may donate your tree to a local park or woodland, if you don't have anywhere suitable to plant it yourself. As the seed grows, ensure that it has the right amount of light, water and is sheltered from any frost. Watch your pot carefully, you might want to take photos or keep a diary to record what happens at each stage. Use all of your senses. *Are there things you see, hear, smell or feel at each stage?*

Perform the poem:

Read the poem again, thinking about the actions and emotions in the poem. *How could you perform the poem to emphasise these?* This could be through physical actions but could also be the way in which you use your voice to emphasise the movements, feelings and actions. Think about the meanings of some of the adjectives and verbs used in the poems, and what these tell us about what and how things are happening, like: **gather**, **loud**, **crinkle**, **spiralling**, **burrowing**. *Will you pace lines or verses differently? Will some be faster or slower than others? Will you change the pitch or volume of your voice?* Consider the senses that are introduced at the start of each verse. Consider how to use your facial expressions and body movements to add to the storytelling, making sure these add too, but don't detract from the meaning of the words and the emotions evoked by the poem. You could record yourself performing and watch this back to consider the effect you have created and the impact of your performance as you watch.

Activate your imagination:

Look outside your window, or even better, take a trip outside to somewhere where you can see plants, animals and trees in your local environment. Take a notebook and pencil with you. Take time to be in the space, taking it in with all of your senses. *What is it like to be there? What do you see, hear, smell? What do things in the environment feel like as you touch them? What is the weather like, and how does this affect you and the other things in the environment? Does the rain cover things in jewels? Does the sun give a glow? Does the wind tickle or surge?*

Think back to the original poem and the imagery created in the words that described how the narrator of the poem was experiencing nature. This might enable you to think of language to describe your own experiences in a poem of your own. You might think of verbs to describe

the actions, like *gather, flutter, crinkle, spiralling, burrowing, surge, feeding, wonder, grow. scuttling, squeezing, carrying,* in the original poem. You might think of how to add description using prepositions or adjectives, such as in the phrases *flutter-songs of summer-end birds, the orange crinkle of leaves spiralling through husky fall air, tiny beasts burrowing inside swells of rough bark.* When you've drafted your verse, think about how you will set it out on the page. *Where will you break the lines? Will you illustrate your verse like Junli Song has in the book?* Share your writing with a friend or family member.

BAMBOOZLED BERRIES

Read and talk about the poem:
Read the poem out loud together and discuss your initial impressions. *What did you notice as you read the poem? How many words beginning with 'b' can you see in the poem? Do you know what they all mean? Which ones might you need to clarify?* Re-read the poem for a second time. Consider the story of the berries in the poem. *What happens to these 'big blue beauts'? How do you think this relates to the title of the poem: Bamboozled Berries? What does the word* **bamboozled** *mean?* Make a prediction based on what you know from the poem, then use a print or online dictionary to check. *Who tricked or fooled the berries? How? Why do you think they did this?*

Explore the concepts:
Consider again why the birds might have 'bamboozled' the berries. *What do we all need to do to be able to survive? What foods are eaten by different creatures? What is similar and different about the foods we eat?* Use this as a chance to talk about different food preferences that people and animals might have. Some are carnivores, some are herbivores and some are omnivores. Look at how this relates to food preferences in humans, some of us eat meat, some are vegetarian and some are vegan. Some people eat foods that reflect the dietary requirements of their cultures and faiths, and some people may have to avoid ingredients that are likely to trigger intolerance or allergies to specific ingredients. You could explore this further by investigating simple food chains, looking at producers and consumers and predators and prey, or where the food we eat comes from, which foods help us develop healthily, which foods are best to eat for our planet as well as ourselves, or how food is distributed – *is this even so that everyone has what they need?*

Perform the poem:

The alliteration in this poem (the repeated consonant sounds at the start of words), make it very tricky to perform, almost like a tongue-twister! Practice reading it through many times to try to get your tongue around the words and read it fluently. As well as focusing on saying the words, think about what they mean. *How will you use your voice to move from the awe and wonder of the beauty of the berries to the drama of them being eaten by the birds?* Think about how you could create the rise and fall in the emotional journey – where you might speed up, where you might slow down, where you might make your voice louder or quieter, where you might take a pause, where lines need to run into each other. Practice a few times to perfect this. Consider how to use your facial expressions and body movements to add to the storytelling, making sure these add to, but don't detract from the meaning of the words and the emotions evoked by the poem. Perform this to a friend or family member and ask for their reactions.

Activate your imagination:

Think about another object you could write a mini drama about. It could be another food-stuff that is eaten by something else, or it could be a household object or another item, which something dramatic happens to. Pick a few items and then see if you can write a mini drama in a sentence, repeating the same initial sound in each word, as Zaro Weil does in her poem. For example, you might have:

A cherished china chicken that gets chucked and chips.

An alluring apple that gets ambushed by an ant with an appetite.

A wonderful wagon that wheels away in a whoosh of winter wind.

Come up with as many mini dramas as you can. Use a print or online dictionary to help you come up with words that start with the same initial sound if this is tricky. If one particularly interests you, you might use other words starting with the same sound to build this up into a longer poem, as Zaro has.

MORNING STILL and MIDNIGHT BRIGHT

Read and talk about the poems:
Read these two poems out loud, one after the other, and talk about them, first separately and then together. *What does each poem make you think about? How does each poem make you feel? What makes you feel this way? What words and phrases stay in your mind after reading? Why do you think this is?* Re-read the poems again and discuss how they are similar and how they are different. *At what time of day is each poem set? What do you notice about the length of the poem and the lines? Why do you think this short form has been used for these poems?* Think about the action that takes place in each poem. *Was this what you expected from this time of day? Why or why not?*

Explore the concepts:
Consider the times of day when each poem is happening. *How is the early morning similar and different to midnight? What sights and sounds might you see and hear at each of these times? How might it feel to experience this time of day?* Open a window or step outside at different times of the day or evening, and on a piece of paper note the time, the different things you see and hear, and how it feels to be there. *What do you notice about the light? The noise? What and who is around? The atmosphere?* Consider all of the times you looked or went outside. *Was there a time of day that you liked best? Why was this?*

Perform the poem:
Re-read the two poems again. Discuss the feelings that each poem evokes in you. *How does it make you feel as you read? Do you think you would perform each poem in the same way, or differently? How might each one be different? Do you think each is a loud poem or a quiet poem; or does it vary? What makes you think this?* Re-read the poem and think about how you might use your voice, facial expressions and body language to create the feelings you felt while reading. Practice a few times to perfect this. Consider how to use your facial expressions and body movements to add to the storytelling, making sure these add to, but don't detract from the meaning of the words and the emotions evoked by the poem. You could record yourself performing and watch this back to consider the effect you have created and the impact of your performance as you watch.

Activate your imagination:
Use the notes you collected from your observations at different times of the day and evening

to create your own short verses about the things you've seen and heard. Read the original poem again to remind yourself of the mood and atmosphere that Zaro Weil created in each of her poems, and the language that she chose to do this. For example, in Morning Still, the stillness is created by the definitive statements, *no clouds drift / no air stirs* – broken by the movement of the *small bird shaking up the quiet light.* There is also lovely opposition here, a small bird doing such a huge action as *shaking up the quiet light,* which might suggest the power of nature. In Midnight Bright, there is also opposition in the fact that midnight, a time when most humans are asleep, is brought to life by *a dozen and one nightingales* and *a full moon. What words and phrases will best describe the mood and atmosphere of the time of day or evening you've chosen? What things that you saw and heard also help to share this?* When you've written your verse you might choose to illustrate it, learning from what Junli Song did in her illustrations.

RECIPE FOR A PERFECT SPRING BIRTHDAY CAKE and DIRECTIONS TO THE NEXT UNIVERSE

Read and talk about the poems:
Begin by reading each poem in turn. *Are these what you would usually expect from a poem? Why or why not? Do these poems remind you of any other kind of writing? What and why?* Explore the similarities between the two poems:

- They both share with the reader how to do or achieve something.

- They are both set out in numbered, sequential steps, each step starting with an imperative verb explaining what to do (e.g. *add, stir, sift, mix, find, follow*) or an adverbial phrase (e.g. *Now carefully navigate, Take a short break*) to show if the time, place, or manner of an action is important and also to shift emphasis and vary the rhythm.

- They both contain precise, technical language appropriate to the subject (e.g. *eight tablespoons, a dash, navigate, Asteroid Belt*).

- They both are anchored in mixing reality and fantasy – the recipe with its fantastical ingredients and the journey that remains fantastical for the majority of humankind.

Read the poems again. *Does one appeal to you more than the other? Which one and why?*

Explore the concepts:

Consider times that you have seen writing like this before. *Have you ever followed a recipe or set of directions or instructions before? Were they written down like this or presented in a different way?* Talk together about how video and audio can be used to share the sequential steps of a process like this, like when we might watch a cooking show or a video on social media to be taken through the steps of creating a recipe or listen to a Satellite Navigation system or watch a virtual tour to be directed to or around places. *Which methods do you find most helpful? Do you like to read and re-read steps, or do you like to see or hear them to be able to follow the steps precisely?* Think about other kinds of instructions that you might have followed, for example to build something, to create something, or to make something work. *How are these different kinds of instructions presented? What makes them easier to follow? What can be challenging? What do they have in common with the instructions given in these poems? What is different?*

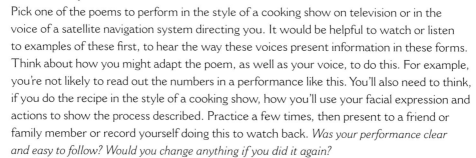

Perform the poem:

Pick one of the poems to perform in the style of a cooking show on television or in the voice of a satellite navigation system directing you. It would be helpful to watch or listen to examples of these first, to hear the way these voices present information in these forms. Think about how you might adapt the poem, as well as your voice, to do this. For example, you're not likely to read out the numbers in a performance like this. You'll also need to think, if you do the recipe in the style of a cooking show, how you'll use your facial expression and actions to show the process described. Practice a few times, then present to a friend or family member or record yourself doing this to watch back. *Was your performance clear and easy to follow? Would you change anything if you did it again?*

Activate your imagination:

Think about a process that you could write a list poem like this about. Maybe you can think of how a Summer, Autumn (Fall) or Winter birthday cake might be made, maybe you could build or make something, maybe you could write instructions for how to play a favourite sport or game. Perhaps you can write directions from your home to another location you know well, or to your own fantastical destination. Use the features from Zaro's original poem to help you with your own writing, such as the numbered sequential steps, the imperative verbs and the adverbial phrases to show if the time, place, or manner of an action is important and also to shift emphasis and vary the rhythm, the precise and technical vocabulary. When you have written them down, give them to someone else to read. *Are they clear and easy to follow? Would they suggest any improvements?*

CLPE is a charity. Support us to continue to provide resources that raise children's engagement and attainment in literacy to schools and parents: https://clpe.org.uk/about-us/donate-support-our-work.

A LITTLE STORY

I still smile out loud when I think back to the little town by the sea where I grew up, with its salt-bewitching smell. I was spellbound by the mad-cap seagulls flying endless loop-de-loops over the waves and treasured the water's fanciful harvest of shells as they rolled onto the beach. I can still feel those damp stubborn grains of sand hiding between my fingers and toes and hear the swing and sway of the limp green-brown seaweed lapping against the shore.

Pretty soon I realised that nothing ever stayed the same on those long stretches of beach. My personal seascape was wild, free, unpredictable and totally magical.

This was the nature I knew first. And loved. It felt like the water and shoreline with all its comings and goings, its great rolls, quiet foams, roughhouse tides, satiny blues and choppy greys were one hundred percent mine.

Or certainly, meant for me.

I grew up needing to be close to all kinds of nature and was always dying to tell my friends and family and anyone who would listen about some enchanted sunset or insect or tree. But to really get my message across the very, very best way I could, I figured I had to write things down.

So I became a poet.

I wrote *I Hear the Trees* to share with you that mind-boggling excitement about Mother Nature, that razz-dazzle, over-the-moon feeling I first experienced all those years ago on my wondrous beach by the sea.

I wish to thank the extraordinary artist Junli Song, who has made
my dreams so thrillingly beautiful on the page. Huge appreciation
to Welbeck and Hachette Children's Books for all their care and support
and I am grateful to Margaret Hope for her wonderful page design
for this title. Huge appreciation to CLPE for the exciting study
notes which accompany this book.

Giant thanks to my dear friend and editor over many years,
the incomparable Judith Elliott and, as ever, to my
supportive family and my husband, Gareth Jenkins.

ABOUT THE AUTHOR AND ILLUSTRATOR

Zaro

Zaro Weil lives on a little farm in southern France. She loves writing and animals (especially dogs 🐶) and trees and oceans and making things up. She has had fantastic fun working with Junli on their third book together, *I Hear the Trees*.

(Other Books By Zaro: *Mud, Moon and Me*, *Firecrackers, Spot Guevara Hero Dog*, *Polka Dot Poems, Cherry Moon* (with Junli) and *When Poems fall from the Sky* (with Junli)

Junli Song lives at Williams College in Massachusetts in the USA, surrounded by trees and mountains. She loves to play with colour and shape, and dreaming up stories of other worlds.

Junli